# Condolences & Eulogies

## Finding the Perfect Words

*In times of loss through death, it eases the*
*grieving to receive perfect words*
*of heartfelt sympathy*
*from loved ones and friends.*

# Condolences & Eulogies

## Finding the Perfect Words

Bettyanne Gillette

Sterling Publishing Co., Inc. New York
A Sterling/Chapelle Book

Chapelle, Ltd.:
>   Jo Packham
>   Sara Toliver
>   Cindy Stoeckl

Editor: Ray Cornia

Editorial Director: Caroll Shreeve
Art Director: Karla Haberstich
Copy Editor: Marilyn Goff
Staff: Burgundy Alleman, Areta Bingham, Emily Frandsen,
Susan Jorgensen, Barbara Milburn, Lecia Monsen, Karmen Quinney,
Kim Taylor, Desirée Wybrow

If you have any questions or comments, please contact:
Chapelle, Ltd., Inc., P.O. Box 9252, Ogden, UT 84409
(801) 621-2777 • (801) 621-2788 Fax
e-mail: chapelle@chapelleltd.com
web site: www.chapelleltd.com

Library of Congress Cataloging-in-Publication Data Available.

10 9 8 7 6 5 4 3 2 1

Published by Sterling Publishing Co., Inc.
387 Park Avenue South, New York, NY 10016
©2003 by Bettyanne Gillette
Distributed in Canada by Sterling Publishing
c/o Canadian Manda Group, One Atlantic Avenue, Suite 105
Toronto, Ontario, Canada M6K 3E7
Distributed in Great Britain by Chrysalis Books
64 Brewery Road, London N7 9NT, England
Distributed in Australia by Capricorn Link (Australia) Pty. Ltd.
P.O. Box 704, Windsor, NSW 2756, Australia
*Manufactured in the United States of America*
*All Rights Reserved*

Sterling ISBN 1-4027-0061-X

*For Dorothy Johnson, my mother*

*Afford me to leave and dream of you, because it's what I'd do. I'd live closely, south of Pasadena, amidst night-blooming jasmine that grows like beanstalks and simple seasons that carry with them a new eternity without loss, but with life, like L.A., with blue skies. Imagine that. Tomorrow, I will go into light and embrace these things.*
                                        *— Malia Spradling*

*The poetry above was written for her grandmother, my mother, who taught me how to yell at Dodger stadium while eating melted Hershey bars, who liked the Beatles when I liked the Beatles, who crocheted hats for AIDS patients, and who showed incredible optimism within the overwhelming world of cancer she was forced to reside in.*

*All the good that I am,*
*came from my mother.*


*Mom, this book is for you.*

# Table of Contents

PART ONE: *Bringing Comfort to the Grieving*            *8–18*

Chapter One:

    Loss Through Death            *8–15*

Chapter Two:

    Defining Perspectives & Expressing Sympathy    *16–18*


PART TWO: *Supportive Condolence Notes*        *19–67*

Chapter Three:

    Writing Condolence Notes            *19–21*

*Chapter Four:*
　　Loss of a Spouse　　　　　　　　　　　*22–28*

*Chapter Five:*
　　Loss of a Child　　　　　　　　　　　　*29–39*

*Chapter Six:*
　　Loss of a Parent or Family Member　　　*40–46*

*Chapter Seven:*
　　Loss of a Friend, Coworker,
　　or Service Person　　　　　　　　　　*47–55*

*Chapter Eight:*
　　Loss Through Suicide　　　　　　　　　*56–60*

*Chapter Nine:*
　　Loss of a Pet　　　　　　　　　　　　　*61–67*

**PART THREE:** *Tributes to the Deceased*　　　*68–94*

*Chapter Ten:*
　　Preparing a Eulogy &
　　Eulogy Examples　　　　　　　　　　　*68–82*

*Chapter Eleven:*
　　Preparing an Obituary &
　　Obituary Examples　　　　　　　　　　*83–88*

**PART FOUR:** *Graceful Words*　　　　　　*89–94*

*Chapter Twelve:*
　　Voiced Words of Comfort　　　　　　　*89–93*

Expressing Sympathy Summary　　　　　　*94*

Index　　　　　　　　　　　　　　　　　*95–96*

## CHAPTER ONE

# Loss Through Death

*G*rief is not a misunderstanding of what a person has, but a clear vision of what he has lost. Losing someone near and dear to us feels like falling off a cliff.

Fortunately, for many grief-laden events that happen in our lives, caring people are often there to help. Yet, some people hesitate to express sorrowful thoughts verbally or in condolence notes. Why? Because they fear that saying the wrong thing will hurt the grieving person even more.

During the process of grief, visits, calls, and condolence notes are not only helpful but necessary because they can soothe the sufferer's pain and give reassurance that, within grief, hope exists and healing is possible.

The right words can be found once the sender understands bereavement and the feelings that come with it—expressions of heartfelt sympathy become clearer and easier to convey.

Visits from close relatives are essential. Yet, visits from people not close to the grieving person can be wearing. This is where cards and letters can serve a great purpose. They can be read at whatever convenient time the bereaved individual chooses, and they let the grieving person know they are loved.

What helps people going through difficult times are words of validation, acknowledging that what they feel is real and part of the grieving process.

To help a loved one through a time of great sorrow, one must first understand what grief is, how it feels, and then take the time to address those feelings in a kind and tactful manner.

The purpose of this book is to create a comfortable environment where sympathetic thoughts can be safely shared. By doing this, the heavy burden of sadness is made lighter.

Writing condolence notes can serve three purposes, it:

• reminds the grieving person that they are not alone. Others have had similar exeriences and can empathize.

• keeps the grieving person connected with life through supportive relationships.

• helps the bereaved person have hope that life will go on and have meaning again.

> *Ah, Hope! what would life be,*
> *stripped of thy encouraging smiles,*
> *that teach us to look behind the dark clouds of today,*
> *for the golden beams*
> *that are to gild the morrow.*
> —*Susanna Moodie*

# When to Express Sympathy

*A* s far as proper etiquette is concerned, time spent or time-liness of sending a heartfelt condolence is not as critical as what is actually said. However, the best time to put thoughts on paper is right after an event has occurred, when feelings are most tender and accessible.

One of the most severe periods of grief tends to occur approximately six weeks after the event, when the reality of the situation settles in. Receiving condolence notes or words of sympathy at this time, when life has returned to normal for all but the grieving person, is comforting because it brings continued reassurance.

Anytime is the best time to send a condolence card because of the person's need to receive one. If a friend were suffering from thirst as a result of a lack of water, would you not continue to provide them with this necessary sustenance? A condolence note is the glass of water that helps to quench the thirsty soul of a grieving person.

# How to Express Sympathy

*W* hen expressing sympathy, sincerity and sensitivity must be top priorities, whether you are writing a condolence note or speaking in person.

Knowing how a grieving person feels may be impossible to discern, but expressing words of support and sorrow are very much within reach.

To assist in finding the proper words of condolence, "The Three Rs," are helpful:

**Recognition**

**Remembrance**

**Reassurance**

• **Recognition:** While mentioning the details of the sorrowful event is not helpful, especially if the loss was of a gruesome nature, acknowledging a grieving person's pain is a kindness that is beneficial:

*Dear Martha,*
*We are so saddened to hear about your father's*
*recent passing.*

• **Remembrance:** Hearing pleasant recollections about the person who passed away is soothing to a bereaved person, as it honors their loved one's life.

*Sam was an example of goodness to his family,*
*friends, and community. He will always be*
*remembered in that light.*

When writing a statement or two of "Remembrance," refrain from using words that tend to "fix things." "God must have needed your mother" makes people feel as though their need of the person was past, that they are not as important to God as the deceased person.

Mention something positive about the grieving person that can be remembered in the form of a reminder. Reminders of a positive attribute give a bereaved person the confidence they need to survive and press forward:

*I immediately thought of how much I admire*
*your resourcefulness and life skills. I am sure*
*they will serve you well in the days ahead.*

• **Reassurance:** Reassuring a bereaved person through offers to help or that your thoughts are with them helps relieve the pressure of feeling alone.

*Our most tender thoughts are with you. If there is anything we can do to help, please don't hesitate to let us know. Just call.*

Reassurance should be genuine and include something from which the grieving person will benefit. "We will check to see what we can do to help on Friday." When reassurance is used in the form of an offer to help, be certain to follow through with that offer.

The three Rs are only to be used as a guideline and should never be mentioned specifically in a letter.

A complete condolence note, using the suggested three Rs, might read as follows:

*Dear Dorothy,*
    (Recognition) *Words cannot express how sorry I am about the recent death of your son.*

    (Remembrance, or in this case, reminder of a positive attribute.) *I have always admired your ability to face each new problem placed before you. Even though this death must seem overwhelming to you and your family, I am certain you will find the strength through your faith to face this great loss.*

    (Reassurance) *I want to help wherever I can, including having you over for dinner soon. I will be in touch on Friday to see how I can help most.*

                *With sincere concern,*
                *Judy*

*Dear Matt,*

*(Recognize) We were sorry to hear of your sister's death. (Remembrance) Marcie was such an incredible woman, who would be proud of the strength you are showing in facing each painful day.*

*(Reassurance) We think about you often and hope the combined strength of those around you will help you feel the love and care you need at this time.*

> *Sincerely,*
> *Terry and Bev*

"You" should only be used when writing inclusive, positive, validating statements like, "Our thoughts are with you," or "We have always admired you and your family."

Recognition, even if it is true, should not be in a form such as, "Your grandmother's dead? Oh my gosh, I can't believe it!" This may be your reaction, but these words are too startling for a person in pain to hear. It is important to remember that printed words always come across more powerfully than spoken ones.

Other points to remember:

• Refrain from letting the person know you've experienced a similar experience, unless your carefully worded supportive comments are meant to identify with their pain and not to minimize or erase it.

• If a friend passes away and you do not know the friend's family, a condolence note should be written to the closest relative of the deceased friend.

• If you do not know the person who passed away (a boss's son, a client's daughter, etc.), but do know his or her relative, the sympathy card should be addressed to the relative you know. If you have heard good things about the deceased second-hand, or have heard positive things about that person directly, you can include it. Some information about the deceased person can be obtained from their obituary.

• When writing a married person who has lost a parent, address the envelope to the person you know and their spouse. If the bereaved person's spouse was close to the in-law, comments in the letter may be addressed to both.

• If the parent of a friend or acquaintance has passed away, the envelope should be addressed to your friend, "Mrs. Allen," with her spouse, "Mr. Allen," written beneath. The card salutation should then read, "Dear Barbara and Tom."

• Preprinted cards are appropriate, as long as personal comments are written inside.

• Sympathy cards should be written in longhand as opposed to typed, unless the sender's handwriting is difficult to read.

• E-mail sympathy cards should not be used as a replacement for handwritten condolence notes.

• Remember to sign the card. Some people become so concerned about how best to express themselves that they forget to sign their name.

## Appropriate Salutations

Sometimes people are hesitant to write a condolence note because they do not know what type of salutation to use when opening their comments. For an informal condolence note to a friend or family member, a first name is acceptable.

For a formal condolence note, the following openings are appropriate:

• A woman may be addressed by Miss, Mrs., Ms., Madam, or a professional title, if it applies. If you are uncertain about what the woman prefers, use Ms.

• A man may be addressed by Mr. or a professional title, if it applies.

• Children may be addressed as Master or Miss.

• A married couple should be addressed by the husband's first and last name, except in cases where the wife has kept her last name or the couple is not married. Then, both of their last names can be used:

*Mr. Johnson and Ms. Parker*

• A couple where one or both have professional titles may be addressed as follows:

*Dr. and Mr. Martin,*

*Drs. Martin,*

*Dr. Bill Martin and Judge Veronica Martin,*

## Complimentary Closes

A condolence note should always include a signature line or complimentary close. The appropriate signature line for an informal condolence note is:

| | |
|---|---|
| *Sincerely,* | *With sincere concern,* |
| *Sincerely yours,* | *With our best wishes,* |
| *Love,* | *For your comfort,* |
| *Your friend,* | *Kind regards,* |
| *In sympathy,* | *With sincere sympathy,* |

When writing a formal condolence note to a person holding a position of authority higher than yours, such as a boss, the correct signature line to use is:

*Respectfully,*

*Respectfully yours,*

CHAPTER TWO

# Defining Perspectives & Expressing Sympathy

## Grief from a Man's Perspective

*M*en generally experience the same steps of grief as women. Some men compartmentalize while others have a need to "fix" things or move on. Men are outwardly less emotional, perhaps reluctant to analyze their feelings. Most keep their thoughts to themselves.

When adults experience trauma, they do not necessarily go through a major personality change. While grief does bring change, basic character traits of the man's personality usually remain the same.

When writing a condolence note to a man, keep his personality in mind, then using the three Rs, develop a tone he will identify with for comfort.

## Grief from a Woman's Perspective

*W*hile men are known for compartmentalizing a painful experience, women may lump all of their feelings into one. They also tend to work through their issues by talking with others, even about very private feelings and thoughts. Because the person a woman most wants to talk with may be a man who doesn't want to talk about painful issues at all, feeling cut off or let down may be a part of their grief. Since their emotions may be closer to the surface, feelings of anger, guilt, and sorrow might well be more intensely expressed.

Such outward displays of feelings certainly are part of the grief process. In addition, some women carry fear and insecurity about what the future might bring. This is why women typically need to be reassured they will survive.

When expressing sympathy or writing a condolence note to a woman, the most genuine approach to take is to keep the woman's unique personality in mind. Then, using words of validation, bring solace to her by using the three steps of recognition, remembrance, and reassurance.

Your own personality should also be present in a condolence note, so the receiver will know your words are sincere.

## *Grief from a Child's Perspective*

*Y*oung children experience grief from their own unique and often naively innocent perspectives. While television, movies, video games, and books expose children to death and loss, the reality is in question because fantasy implies no one really dies. Characters get back up and walk away, particularly in cartoons and the animated films and videos.

The reality of a truly life-altering death within a family, neighborhood, or community can be emotionally and mentally paralyzing to a child. Children usually lack experience in dealing with true tragedy. Young children need reassurance that they will be loved and cared for by nurturing people in the future. Concerns about the needs for changing home, school, and friends must be addressed quickly in a reassuring manner.

## Grief from an Adolescent's Perspective

*T*eenagers struggle to establish their place in life; many reactions result, one of which is their need to belong. Sometimes they fear appearing different because of a perceived threat of being ostracized from "the group," especially in situations where they feel little or no control.

During this time of discovering who they are, death, loss, or change can be especially hard for them to manage. They may experience confusing feelings during the grieving process. Foreign and overwhelming thoughts can result. Pain may be shifted to other outlets. Anger can also be common as attempts are made to deny or reject acceptance of a death.

## Grief from a Young Adult's Perspective

*E*ven though young adults can be more independent, this doesn't necessarily mean they have learned how to cope in times of great sorrow over the loss of a family member or close friend. The death of a celebrity they admire can bring grief and a confusing sense of fear that others more dear to them could abandon them as well.

Most young adults still lack the experience needed to realize they have the tools necessary to emotionally move their lives

forward in a positive way. As a result, they need support, and, like everyone else, they love to receive correspondence. For college students away from home for the first time, depending on the support of new friends, concern in words can be their greatest light and comfort.

## CHAPTER THREE

# Writing Condolence Notes

*P*ut yourself in the recipient of your note's place. Trust your instincts, listen to yourself emotionally, and then write every sincere word you believe the bereaved person would want to hear.

For those people with whom you have a close relationship, you may suggest a specific day or week in the near future when you will call to make certain they are well and to offer support or assistance. A person's needs change with time. A true friend will keep in touch and renew their offers of action to make the grieving person's life easier.

Honor the characteristics of the person when writing a condolence note. Interact with the grieving person in a way that reflects their personality. Some people deflect pain through humor; gently joking with them is appropriate. Others take most things seriously. Some choose not to talk about things which are unpleasant or difficult. Some want to be left alone to work through their grief themselves. Equally important is the personal follow-up to the offer of help in your note.

Monumental loss causes many painful emotions to surface. At some point, a grieving person finds it hard to believe anyone has ever gone through this before. As a result, isolation may set in as the bereaved person becomes unable to identify with people not in pain. Receiving a condolence note helps by keeping a bereaved person connected to those around him or her and relieves feelings of loneliness.

# Condolence Notes Do's and Don'ts

**Do**

1. Do write a condolence note.

2. Do speak from the heart.

3. Do acknowledge the person's grief.

4. Do keep your comments simple and short.

5. Do give kind remembrances of the object of the loss.

6. Do give positive comments about the grieving person's strengths.

7. Do offer help. If you know them well enough, be specific with your offers by action, or suggest and ask for an okay.

8. Do speak in present-tense. "We are" instead of "We were" gives immediacy and intimacy to your words.

9. Do mention if a financial gift or contribution has been made in their name and to what fund.

**Do not**

1. Do not refrain from writing for fear of saying the wrong thing. If everyone did this, the grieving person would be alone in their grief.

2. Do not send a lengthy letter. The mind of a grieving person is filled with so much grief that sifting through lengthy letters may be emotionally exhausting, if not impossible.

3. Do not give long speeches, profound lessons, or guilt-ridden regrets. This is not a time for you, but for the comfort of the grieving person.

4. Do not try to replace their grief with clichés like, "Look on the bright side," or with situations worse than their own.

5. Do not talk about other subjects unrelated to their grief.

6. Do not dwell on the cause of grief.

7. Do not forget to follow through with offers to help.

8. Do not mention the amount of a financial contribution.

## How to Use Condolence Note Examples

*T*here is nothing more important than receiving words of encouragement at a time when a person feels their world has been completely shattered. When the need is pressing and emotions on the part of a person writing a condolence message may be as intense as the bereaved person who will receive it, it is helpful for the writer to have examples for what to say.

You, as the writer of a heartfelt expression of sympathy, can be the comforter for a bereaved person who is dear to you; works with you; lives in your neighborhood; or attends social, professional, or religious organizations you share.

The following chapters present expressions of sympathy intended as guides for the writer and support in being sensitive and sincere. Borrowing a phrase or a paragraph that rings true to the needs of the person you are addressing may be helpful to the writer in expressing thoughts, and beneficial to the reader.

These expressions of sympathy are organized in chapters by topic according to the relationship of the deceased to the bereaved person who will be receiving the condolence note.

Some types of loss can be so devastating, as in the death of a spouse or a child, that an immediate response helps a bereaved person know that they are not alone in their grief process.

Locate the heading most applicable to your situation and need, then make use of these personally expressed, sincere words of comfort to help another deal with loss through death.

## CHAPTER FOUR

# *Loss of a Spouse*

*W*hen a spouse passes away, in addition to the expected feelings of grief mentioned in Chapter One, the following individual reactions can occur:

- Hopelessness

- Emotional paralysis

- Anxiousness over financial pressures

- Fearfulness about social adjustments

The death of a spouse can be expected or sudden, followed by an excruciatingly painful adjustment that can affect several areas of a bereaved person's life.

The surviving spouse can feel a deep sense of loss of the present as they become plucked from the life in which they recently felt so secure. The more dependent or close the married couple were before the death, unexpected or not, and the more lengthy the relationship, the more deeply the grief will be experienced by the surviving spouse. It is also understandable for a newlywed faced with loss through death to experience extreme grief.

Addressing these concerns as specifically as you are able will help the grieving person tremendously. Easing the fears of any spouse left bereaved by the loss of their partner is a kindness that will be welcomed, provided you approach your message and offer of support in a manner that fits their personality. Keep in mind the topics likely to be of concern to the grieving spouse will help you know what to include in your condolence note.

## Loss of a husband, condolence to a wife:

Dear Kathy,

I am so sorry to hear of Rick's passing. How incredibly difficult this sorrowful time must be for you and your family.

May you feel him near in the flowers he planted each spring, hear him in the roar of a UCLA football crowd, and see him in the roll of his lucky number seven. He will be greatly missed by all who knew him.

My heart goes out to you in your pain. I'll be in touch week after next to invite you out for an evening. We'll talk only if you feel ready to. Perhaps a walk in the park or a new film would distract you for a couple of hours. Please know that many people are thinking about you at this time.

Love,
Miranda

Dear Mrs. Thompson,

I am sorry to hear about the passing of your husband, Floyd. You always spoke highly of him. I'm certain he was a great man because great men marry great women.

May the peace of a treasure chest of special Floyd memories comfort you now and in the days ahead.

Respectfully,
Sandy

## Loss of a husband, condolence to a wife:

Dear Cindy Ann,

The tragic news of Jack's death while arresting a criminal is heartbreaking. Don and I have trouble talking about the dangers policemen like our husbands face every day on the job. It is news we never want to hear. We are so sorry to imagine the loss you and the children must feel and the fears you have expressed for their future without Jack.

Please know that we will always be here for your family. We'll take the boys to practice and ball games like always, and you can sit with us at the park as you often did.

Don has started a collection for Zach and Nick's education to help you fulfill Jack's dreams of college for them. Whatever else we can do to comfort or to help, please don't hesitate to ask. If we can't handle it ourselves, we'll help you find someone who can.

Don will mow the lawn after work this week and next, and help you find a way to keep it under control. We all love you. You aren't facing Jack's loss alone.

Love,

Mindy and Don

Our Dear Charlene,

Your phone call about Ben's passing touched us beyond words. We are honored you would call personally, and of course we'll help by singing at his memorial.

His favorite hymns are a fine idea. We'll begin preparing immediately and record them for you as a keepsake.

Love, Susie and Rich

Dear Tonya,
   Your sister called us to say Les had died in a hiking fall. When we lived next door to one another, Les was such a good neighbor who had fun and always shared his tools. Though we can't be close to pay our respects and help you physically now, we would like to send a contribution to Karen's education fund or to help financially in some other way.
   Please call or drop us a note when you're able. We hold you in our prayers and in our hearts as always.

Love, Elizabeth and Peter

## Loss of a wife, condolence to a husband:

Dear Chip,

There are no words that can express the sadness I feel for you, buddy. I came by as soon as I heard about Lindsay's accident. The neighbors said you never left her side and that she had passed. Lindsay was my idea of an ideal wife and none of us guys will forget her.

I'll take care of walking Champ or we can do it together. Tell me what else you need.

Josh

Dear Alec,

Debbie's loss has been a shock to us but to you most of all. We will help with the children, either in your home or ours while you do everything you need to do at this unexpected time. We've enclosed our cell number. Keep it with you and call at any hour. We're here for all of you.

Love,
Jenny and Kirk

Dear Rob,

It seems impossible that Linda is no longer with us. It's probably little comfort at the moment, but believe me we are grieving with you.

Linda's creative spirit and classy character have influenced all of us lucky enough to be your close friends. Her handmade greeting cards, that we framed for the living room, are more treasured than ever.

We'll bring Aunt Nina's pies to her wake, help clean up, and Cid and I will take care of mowing and trimming your lawn as long as you need us to. Whatever else we can do, you have only to ask. We love you.

CJ and Donna

Brad,

You've always had the biggest heart of anybody in our family. It doesn't seem fair that "The Bear" is the one needing our hugs, but I bet you do. Liz and I go way back, but you were her hero, her best friend, and she said she was as crazy about you after seven years as your wife as on your first date. I'll miss her with you.

You know I'll take my godmother status for Timmy very seriously.

Affectionately in Sorrow, Angie

## Loss of a wife, condolence to a husband:

*Dear Bill,*

*Eddie and I are so sorry to hear about Edna's passing. It never matters how long you've expected something, the loss of your dearest loved one and friend is always more devastating than one could have imagined.*

*We know you've been as devoted to her emotional and physical support as any husband could have been. The void of not having her to care for hour by hour must feel unbearable.*

*If we can be of help and comfort to you, we hope you'll feel free to ask. We're quite sincere about that, Bill. We're only a phone call away.*

*When I lost my Jeff, it took me a long time to recover, so don't expect your grief to ease quickly. It rarely does. Give yourself time. Let your friends and family help you adjust. We all care.*

*With sincere sympathy,*

*Louise and Eddie*

CHAPTER FIVE

# Loss of a Child

𝒯he death of a child is perhaps the most difficult of all grief experiences. Parents expect that their children will outlive them. When an infant or a young person dies, the magnitude of this event can be so enormous and unacceptable that it can scarcely be absorbed. Not only is the present taken, the future is gone as well, making it feel as though an entire lifetime of dreams and expectations of shared events has been lost.

Age of the child does not make a difference in the degree of sorrow, nor does a miscarriage, a stillbirth or a terminal illness as opposed to an accidental death. Loss of a child of any age is intensely and uniquely painful.

Some feel if a death is expected, the loss might be lessened, but this is not true. Caregiving can be so intense in the months preceding an ailing child's death that the void left in its place can be nearly unbearable.

Expressing words like, "God must have needed your baby" or "Your baby has gone to a better place," or "Your child is much happier now," does not reassure the grieving person.

Recognizing the loss, remembering strengths, and reassuring through offers to help will aid in supporting and showing your genuine sympathy to a parent who has lost a child.

## Loss of an infant through miscarriage, condolence to parents:

Dear Stephanie and Todd,

I know how much you wanted and anticipated the birth of your baby boy. I believe he will always be a part of you—in your heart, mind, thoughts, and dreams. He gave you expanded hope and love, gifts you will both cherish.

My heart goes out to you at this time. May you receive deep peace and comfort.

Sincerely,
Janice

Dear John and Ellen,

I just heard about your sad news and wish there were something I could say to ease the sorrow you must feel.

I hope to see you both soon. Know that I am thinking about you and remembering you in my prayers. I am hopeful that each day will bring more moments of joy and comfort as you work through adjusting to the miscarriage of your baby.

With sincere concern,
Bernice

Dear Theresa and Mike,

To experience the miscarriage of your eagerly awaited baby must fill you with great sorrow.

What a strong couple you are to face all you have experienced the last couple of months. I wish you well in the recovery of your good health and in the months ahead.

Sincerely,

Faye

Dear Heather,

I know how much you and Bob wanted this baby and I am so sorry your dream was not able to come true. Remembering how difficult my miscarriage was, it seemed so much changed so quickly. Rest helps, so does talking, and even crying as life painfully moves forward. Please know how much I care for you at this time.

I will call next week to see how you are doing and if you want someone to listen who understands a bit of what you feel.

Sincerely,

Darla

## Loss of an infant through miscarriage, condolence to parents:

Dear Mark,

We can still remember how excited you were when you came in the office and told us your wife was expecting. We are sorry your baby did not grow to full term and birth.

Please know we're thinking about you and Bonnie and want to do whatever we can to help. If you need an afternoon or two away from the office, we would be more than happy to arrange it. Just let us know which days would be best.

Respectfully,

Tina, Wanda, and Barbara

---

Dear Kimbra and Jef,

Our hearts are full of love for you, sorrow for the miscarriage of your baby, and gratitude that you, Kimbra, are in good health. We can only guess at the bewildering feelings of loss you are both experiencing, and we're grateful that you have one another for comfort.

We will have you over to dinner as soon as you feel like company.

Love,

Caroll and AB

## Loss of an infant through stillbirth, condolence to parents:

Dear Susan and Todd,

We want you to know how deeply we care for you and share your pain at the stillbirth of your baby.

Words are so inadequate to express our love and concern for you at this time of your loss. We'll help with whatever you may need in the way of meals, shopping, housekeeping, or yard work—and of course—hugs.

Love,
Julie and Don

Dear Nancy and Phil,

I have cried many times for you and your loss. Phil told me Marya was a beautiful baby. I am sorry your precious infant's life could not be sustained.

God give you both the strength you need to make it through such a difficult time. Even though I live far away, I will be in touch often to make certain you have at least one more listening ear.

Love always,
Elizabeth

## Loss of an infant through death, condolence to parents:

B&R

Dear Tracy and Jim,

The five days your family spent together holding Emily are days I am certain you will keep in your hearts forever. We are sorry your time with Emily was so short and know that her life will remain with you through brief but all the more precious memories.

May you feel our thoughts of love and concern and know that our helping hands are nearby. We'll call before we grocery shop to see what you may need with all of the company coming from out of town for funeral services.

Your friends,

Bryan and Rebecca

---

Dear Anthony and Nicole,

We've just heard of little Arla's passing and can barely comprehend what feelings you must have. We are so sorry that corrective surgery didn't improve her chances for survival and recovery.

Sometimes there isn't expertise or time enough for making things work out the way we pray they will. We hold you in our hearts through this time of such unexpected pain and loss. Please know that we offer the comfort and support with time and effort that you may imagine from friends who love you dearly.

Love,
Nick and Carla

**Loss of an ailing child through death, condolence to parents:**

Dear Don and Delaney and family,

Our family cares so much for yours and we are so saddened to hear about the loss of your dear, sweet Gina. She was an adorable child. She will be greatly missed for her cheerful smile amidst her many health challenges and her pride in twirling in dress-up skirts.

Our lives have been truly blessed because of her and our friendship with each of you. May the peace and comfort of the many who love you be in your heart.

Sincerely,
Ned and Wendy

---

Dear Steve and Karen,

Timothy was such a courageous child who lived a joyful life amidst years of sickness. He is our hero for the smile he wore and the sunshine he spread in spite of every ordeal he had to endure.

We will miss him and are determined to keep his legacy with us as we strive to take upon us his two greatest attributes: kindness and generous love.

Let us help wherever we can. Our love and thoughts are with you.

Love,
Scott, Maryann, and family

## Loss of an ailing child through death, condolence to parents or grandparents:

Dear Sheila and Art,

Our hearts go out to you in the loss of Angela.

We had hoped with you that she would survive her accident and surgery. Some things are out of our hands and we have to surrender our anguish to a higher power. That certainly doesn't mean Angie's loss isn't going to hurt you and all of us for a long time.

We will remember her zest for life and her joy in making her friends laugh with all the ways she always thought of to have fun and include everyone.

Her laughter will always echo in our hearts.

We love and support you in sincerest sympathy,

Grieving with you,

Tony and Marsha

## Loss of a grandchild, condolence to grandparents:

Dear Russ and Merilee,

We are sorry to hear about Allison's and Jamie's baby. How hard it must be to experience such a painful loss and to want so much to ease your children's suffering.

We know how much you love your grandchildren. That's the kind of devoted grandparents you have always been. We grieve for your sorrow, knowing the special plans you've looked forward to.

You are in our thoughts and the focus of our prayers. May peace and comfort abide with you soon.

Love always,
Al and Louise

---

Dear Joyce and Tim,

When we heard of your grandson Brad's death, our shock was staggering. Though we know our words are totally inadequate to the task of easing your despair, we want you to know how much we both wish for our prayers and love to bring you some measure of comfort.

In sincere sympathy,

Mindy and Joe

**Loss of a child through accidental death, condolence to parents, grandparents, or godparents:**

Dear Jim and Francis,

We cannot imagine how difficult it must be for you in the loss of Kinter. Sometimes after all we do, something still happens to make us lose what we work so hard to keep safe.

We have always looked to you both as examples of strength and courage. How we wish we could repay your example with some comfort, but feel totally inadequate in this circumstance.

You are in our prayers. Kinter was lucky to have you for parents. We're certain she enriched your lives in ways that will remain dear to you both.

In deepest sympathy,

Bob and Nancy

**Loss of a child through kidnapping and death, condolence to parents or grandparents:**

Dear Jolene and David,

We can't convey how deeply sorrowful we are at the news that bears out your worst fears, and ours, for Angie. We had hoped and prayed with you for her safe return, and cannot imagine the agony of worry you and your family have experienced these last few weeks.

We hope you can find comfort in our deepest sympathy and love, now and always.

Ben and Treeny

## Loss of an older child through death, condolence to grandparents, parents, or godparents:

Dear Bonnie and Rafe,

We've been on an extended trip out West and just learned of your daughter's heart attack and sudden passing during our absence. Such an unexpected happening for a young mother took us by surprise.

You must be overwhelmed with grief and the daily routine of details for two young children. We are touched by your decision to care for Katy and Tip, until they go to live with your daughter Amanda this summer. You can be proud of the children you have brought up by your example to be compassionate and committed to family.

Please allow us to help. Your grandchildren are welcome to come and play when ours are visiting. They all met at the Grant reunion last year, so they're not complete strangers. We visit a round of museums, movie houses, and roller rinks throughout the winter to entertain ours, so perhaps we could join forces and encourage friendships between the four kids. We'd be happy to plan an outing later in the month that works around your plans with Katy and Tip.

Our thoughts and prayers for comfort are with you and your entire family in this difficult time.

With deepest sympathy,
Glen and Carolyn

CHAPTER SIX

# Loss of a Parent or Family Member

*C*hildren expect their parents will always be there. When a parent, beloved grandparent, sister, brother, or dear relative passes away, a child can feel cheated or even abandoned because their special grown up will not be there in the future to share in daily living, to spend holidays with, or to attend special events they would have shared. The intensity of the loss can be increased with the degree of dependency of the child.

Upon the death of one or both parents, children also may feel the reality of their own mortality. They grieve in association with the past they shared with their parent or other family member, and they may feel abandonment and fear for how they will be taken care of literally or emotionally in the future.

Tender, nurturing words from loved ones and close friends are essential at a time when someone loses a parent or grandparent, and will help to console the heart of a grieving son or daughter, sister or brother, niece or nephew, aunt or uncle, of any age.

Depending upon the degree of commitment or bonding, relationships by marriage and other than blood, such as unmarried or same-sex couples, may cause similar loss concerns:

- fear of never being happy again.

- pain from social adjustments.

- stress from financial pressures.

The death of a person or the people who gave us life creates a uniquely deep and intense pain for children, whether that parent was there for us or not during our time together in life.

**Loss of a father, condolence to a boy or young man:**

Dear Todd,

I am so sorry that your father has passed away. You were lucky to have such a great father who not only spent time with you, but with all your friends too. He will be greatly missed by all of us, but will be remembered forever. You are fortunate to have inherited so many of your father's kind and fun-loving qualities.

I hope you know and take comfort in how much you mean to your sports friends in the city league.

Your coach and friend,

Brad

Dear Richey,

Your dad may be gone, but he won't be forgotten by anyone who ever had the opportunity to work with him or become his friend. I'll always remember how patient he was at teaching us the skills for our Boy Scout merit badges.

I'll have a set made of the photos from our winter endurance retreat, so you can enjoy remembering that fantastic survival ice cave you and your dad made together.

In sympathy, your buddy,
Andy

**Loss of a father, condolence to a daughter:**

*Dear Sandy,*

*You may not be able to feel anything but pain right now at your dad's passing, even though it was a relief of his suffering. We hope it comforts you to know that his miseries were eased by your tender care and deep devotion to helping him through every turn of his medical treatment.*

*It is a rare thing these days to observe a daughter's sacrifice to her own dreams and other responsibilities in order to be of help to one of her parents. You brought him great comfort when he needed it most.*

*We always wish we had done more for our parents, but your dad, Bill, always claimed that he had the best daughter in the world.*

*We agree with him!*

*Love,*

*Aunt Margaret and Uncle Jake*

## Loss of a mother, condolence to a son:

Dear Ernest,

It seems that one never knows exactly what to say at a time like this. I want to say just the right words to tell you how sorry I am for the loss of your mother, to let you know that there isn't anything I wouldn't do to help, and to promise that there are reasons for all of life's passages.

I didn't know your mother but I do know that she was a wonderful woman because she raised a son who is loyal, compassionate, and successful. A son who honors her family's name with grandchildren and great-grandchildren, a sterling career, and admirable community service.

May you find peace in your time of sorrow and joy in the memories of the days when the two of you were together. I'm certain she was as proud of you as you have always seemed to be of her.

My prayers are with you,
Charlene

Dear George,

I was so sorry to hear that your mother passed away. There is nothing I can say to ease your pain at her passing, but I wanted you to know how much I wish there were a way to bring you comfort. When you feel like talking, please call or come by.

Sincerely, Alex

## Loss of a mother, condolence to a daughter:

*Dear Lindsay,*

*I am saddened at the passing of your dear mother. For many years, your mother and I sat next to each other in the church choir. We all loved her terrific sense of humor, her kindness, and her compassionate nature. At the personal troubles of our members, Marlene gave each a healthier way to look at them and go on. We shall all miss her.*

*I sincerely hope that you can draw upon her many fine qualities to ease your own grief at her passing. She was so proud of your every accomplishment and so patient about giving you room to grow into the young woman you are. We all admired her so.*

*Every time our choir sings "Nearer My God to Thee," I shall think of my dear friend, your mother, for she expressed many times how that hymn was her favorite.*

*With deep affection,*
*Donna Trimble*

*Dear Yolanda,*

*I know how much you loved your mother and will miss her. I am sorry that her days with you have been shortened.*

*I hope peace and comfort will be yours, and that memories of your mother will fill your heart and help you feel her near forever.*

*Sincerely,*
*Debra*

**Loss of a brother, condolence to a man:**

Dear Sam,

I'm so sorry to hear of your loss. Your brother Ron was the most fun of any guy on our bowling league team. He never cared how lousy I bowled, as long as I showed up on time and took my turn to score in good nature. He hated that scoring the numbers part and had more jokes about bad score excuses than anyone I've ever met.

Brad wouldn't want you or any of us to grieve for long, because he truly believed that he had a good place to go "When his number was up." There's no doubt in my mind that he's running something for fun upstairs and looking down on you and all of us with thumbs up, the way he did when anyone on our team got a strike.

I will always remember Brad with a smile.

Kindest regards,

Joe Sumner

**Loss of a brother, condolence to a woman:**

Dear Julie,

I want you to know how sorry I am about the death of your brother. You were such a good sister to him. I can still remember all of the fun you two had together. May the great love you shared remain to comfort you always.

Love,
Verda

## Loss of a sister, condolence to a woman:

Dear Eileen,

When we heard about your sister Shiela's death, we were overcome with sorrow for you and for her husband and young family. Shiela was a devoted sister, wife, and mother who will be missed.

We have sent a donation to American Bank in her name, and will be in touch to see what we can do to comfort you.

Our thoughts are with you,
Betty and George

## Loss of a stepparent, condolence to a man:

Dear James,

Your stepfather, Les, was so devoted to you and your mother. You will be blessed forever because of his many kindnesses. Even in his last days in the nursing home, I remember him giving a laugh here and a helping hand there. He will be missed by many, which speaks volumes about the kind of thoughtful person he was.

I am mindful of your sorrow and want to help wherever I can. Perhaps you would like my help, at some point, on a memory album of photos and his letters. I'll get in touch next month to see if you feel up to it emotionally.

Your friend, Roberta

## CHAPTER SEVEN

# Loss of Friend, Coworker, or Service Person

*M*ost people have dear friends who are as important to them as any family member. If a friend such as this dies, there is an immense sense of loss. A person may face a dramatic change in lifestyle when a friend dies because the two of them have shared so much of their everyday life,

including perhaps activities, organizations, transportation, vacations, job responsibilities, or even business partnerships.

When writing a condolence note to someone who has lost a friend, keep in mind the type of relationship the two people have enjoyed. Many close friends do not see each other for long periods of time, but the loss that is felt can be as deep as for friends who interact daily. Coworkers and service persons have filled valued roles in the lives of some people and they may have developed sustaining friendships over time as well.

With dear friends, it is usually the way they make each other feel important, needed, appreciated, and supported that defines their value and closeness to each other. Women may confide their most vulnerable secrets to one another from an early age, while boys and men may define their bond with other boys or men in terms of shared activities and interests. In each case, when a person loses a friend of great value, there is great loss.

Special friends cannot be replaced. A person may be able to make new friends, but the bond a person makes with a best friend as an individual is special and cannot be duplicated.

## Loss of a friend, condolence to a man:

Jack,

I just heard about Ted and wanted you to know I was thinking of you. He was a good friend and I know you will miss him.

I have to smile when I think of Ted and how hard he tried to beat you at raising some big roses. He must have spent $500.00 per year on all his surefire rose-growing schemes. He was proud to be best friends with the "champion rose grower." You will never find anyone else who could lose to you as gracefully as Ted because your friendship came first.

Take care. I'll see you soon.

Al

Hey George,

Tough times and there's no words that can ease the loss of your long-time buddy PK. Tom and I are going up to the lake next weekend and would like your company. Please come. It's been too long since we all took off and let the world take care of itself, while we concentrated on extracting all the fish from the lake. Grab your gear and join us. You know PK would have said "just go for it."

If you can't make it this time, I'll get in touch and we will find something else you'd rather do on another weekend.

Frank

## Loss of a friend, condolence to a woman:

Dear Kathleen,

We are saddened to hear that your best friend Danielle has passed so suddenly. We know you two have been anticipating a long vacation together in Europe for months. Her accident was a shock to us all.

Knowing that you have been dear friends from child to adulthood, her loss may seem overwhelming to accept. We are certain she will live on in your many precious memories of the years of fun you've shared together.

With love,
Margaret and Andy

Gwen,

I wanted to write and tell you how sorry I feel about Jane. I know this must be hard for you because you both were so close. Friends like that cannot be replaced.

Recently, I was remembering how Jane made that horrible cake for the church dinner. It was the only kitchen mistake I ever knew her to make. I laughed when I remembered the pastor's face as he took a big bite. If you run onto Jane's recipe for that cake, let me know. We could make it together for Jeff's next birthday, if you like.

Love,
Sandy

## Loss of friends, condolence to a couple:

*Dear Tommy and Anne,*

*Ned and I are keeping you close in our prayers and thoughts. You are not alone in your grief.*

*We know what dear friends you were with Carl and Cynthia. Our weekly gourmet bridge club the four of you started with that first masters' table years ago will remain a tribute to your foursome and friendship.*

*The shock of losing them both so suddenly in the accident is nearly overwhelming to all of us. We can only imagine your sense of personal loss and hope that you know how deeply we share this sad time with the two of you.*

*Our club met quickly last night and decided to host the family meal following the funeral service, and we'll set up and clean up. No doubt you will have picked up the message to that effect by the time you receive this note.*

*We all wonder what you two would think of renaming our bridge club in Carl's and Cynthia's memory.*

*Our sincere condolences,*

*Nick and Dianne*

**Loss of a coworker, condolence from two men to a man:**

Andy,

We're so sorry to hear that your office mate Jason could not be revived after his climbing accident. You've talked of him so often over the three years you guys have worked together, that we feel like we knew him, too.

It's going to be tough working on that big computer analysis program without him, when you were used to problem solving together. We know the two of you were a real team asset to your company and that you took pride in coming up with innovative ideas.

Whenever you feel you're up against another one of those "big blank walls" you guys would tell us about, you'll just have to imagine what Jason would have suggested. Who knows, maybe he'll continue to keep coming right on through for you like always.

We deeply regret your sadness at this time.

Harm and Jim

## Loss of coworker, condolence to a couple:

Dear June and Steven,

We cannot imagine the feelings you must carry in your heart at this time at Natalie's passing. She was the most competent of secretaries and cheerful person in our office. We know how much you both enjoyed your friendship of many years.

Our thoughts are with you, now and always.

With kindest regards,
Megan and Seth

## Loss of business partner, condolence to a couple:

Dear Bruce and Linda,

We heard about your business partner Adam's passing. Knowing he was also a special friend, we are certain that you and your business staff will miss him very much.

With your combined strength, we hope you'll be able to accept his loss and continue your business activities during the resulting reorganization with a minimum of stress.

The changes Adam's loss will cause in your day-to-day activities may leave you wanting a relaxing place to have dinner that you don't have to prepare. Please join us often.

Sincerely,
Carolyn and Gary

## Loss of a service person, condolence to a woman or man:

Dear Sarah,

I was sorry to hear about your assisted-living companion Alice's passing and the difficult changes it will make in your living arrangements. I hope you know how much you are loved. May this love continue to be shown to you through the many offers from people wanting to help—including my own.

For the remainder of this month, my sister Connie and I will come and take care of your weekly laundry and Sunday evening meals. No one can replace Alice in your heart, but someone will be found who is just right to assist you in your apartment. Until then, you won't be left without support.

Thinking of you,
Cindy

Dear Fred,

The shock I feel can't compare to what you must be feeling with your housekeeper Mindy gone. If you want to talk or get out for a change of scenery, bring the dogs and they can play with Buster in the backyard while we catch a football game on TV.

It's a hard time, but you don't have to go through it by yourself. You'e been there for me. I'm here for you.

Your friend,
Tom

## Loss of a service person, condolence to a business owner:

Dear Karen,

Words will not express the sorrow we feel for you at this time. May your many friends and staff be there to help you through the loss of your senior hairstylist, and may we be counted among them.

We'll contact the salon receptionist and wait until you can comfortably reschedule us. We're sending a little remembrance to Marion's favorite charity.

Your friends, Tamara and daughter Tonya

## Loss of a service person, condolence to an employer:

Dear Jesse,

We are sorry to hear your housekeeper, Iris, was involved in an accident that took her life. We know that over the years of her faithful service, you two had become dear friends. She seemed to enjoy making life easier for you since your hip replacement.

It's a difficult time for you with everything you're used to her taking care of now having to be arranged for differently.

We are thinking about you and hope you will know how much we want to help during this grieving and readjustment period, until someone else can be found to help you. You have always been special to us. We'll keep in touch so you don't have to be the first one to call.

Love,
Bruce and Marla

## Loss of a service person, friend, condolence to a woman:

Dear Chloe;

Sandy and Herb just told me that your hairdresser, Tiffany, at Compton's passed away. I know that you've had her color and style your hair for a dozen years. You must be so sad because I know you loved the great chats you two had several times a month and the way she did your hair to please you.

I'm sure you find it difficult to imagine a better relationship for skill and friendship that made you feel so special whenever you had an appointment with Tiffany. I'm certain she looked forward to talking with you, too, every time you went to her for a styling.

In sympathy,
Alane

## Loss of a service person, friend, condolence to a couple:

Dear Herb and Joanie,

Ty and I learned at bridge club that your yard man Clancy passed away last week. He's been making your lawn and gardens the envy of the neighborhood for so long that he seemed like a part of your family.

We're so sorry for your loss and hope that you are managing the shock of his being gone. Clancy was one of the most gracious of men, not to mention an expert on roses and lilies. We shall miss him too.

Dorothy and Rod

## CHAPTER EIGHT

# Loss Through Suicide

*L*oss through suicide is one of the most devastating forms of grief to address in words of comfort. Many of the standard reactions to death seem to be more intense when they come with the sudden and traumatic death associated with someone who has taken their own life. Great care should be given to every word expressed. In this case, a few heartfelt words sincerely expressed are the most appropriate condolence.

When dealing with this issue, the three Rs of recognition, remembrance, and reassurance can still be used. However, a condolence note should *begin with reassurance* to let the bereaved person know, first and foremost, that they are not alone in their grief. People who commit suicide may trigger a chain reaction of guilt and remorse on the part of their loved ones. The clues they may put together after someone's death can perhaps indicate a depth of despair family and friends underestimated and come too late for the intervention they would have eagerly provided.

The loved ones of a spouse or adolescent who takes their own life are particularly anguished and may be filled with not only grief, but guilt, thinking surely there must have been some way to have prevented such a tragedy.

Consider your words carefully when writing a condolence note to one who has lost another through the tragedy of suicide. Do not put yourself in a psychiatric or pastoral role with the bereaved unless you are truly an experienced professional. Speak from your heart simply and be kind.

## Loss through suicide, condolence to parents:

Dear Steve and Alana,

You are in our thoughts and prayers daily and we want to do whatever we can to help you at this time.

Your daughter Sarah was such a sensitive, introspective, good person. We are deeply sorry to hear her personal struggles overwhelmed her.

Please know that our most sincere prayers are with you, that you will not be alone in your grief, and that there are countless numbers of people who love and care about you. We all loved Sarah and will hold her dear always.

Sincerely,
Mike and Nina

Dear Braden and Linda,

Words cannot express the sorrow we feel for you at this time. To lose a child in such a painful way must feel nearly unbearable.

Please know that we are mindful of your grief for Joey and want to send peace and comfort your way. We pray that you will feel the great love and warmth that surrounds you at this difficult time.

Your friends,
Malia and Darcy

## Loss through suicide, condolence to parents:

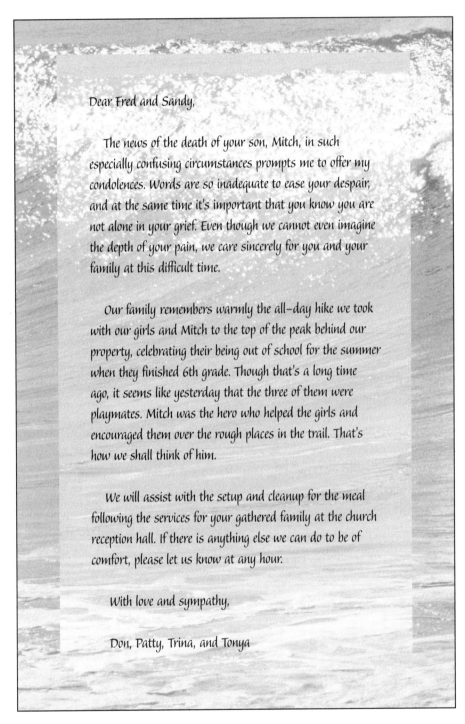

Dear Fred and Sandy,

The news of the death of your son, Mitch, in such especially confusing circumstances prompts me to offer my condolences. Words are so inadequate to ease your despair, and at the same time it's important that you know you are not alone in your grief. Even though we cannot even imagine the depth of your pain, we care sincerely for you and your family at this difficult time.

Our family remembers warmly the all-day hike we took with our girls and Mitch to the top of the peak behind our property, celebrating their being out of school for the summer when they finished 6th grade. Though that's a long time ago, it seems like yesterday that the three of them were playmates. Mitch was the hero who helped the girls and encouraged them over the rough places in the trail. That's how we shall think of him.

We will assist with the setup and cleanup for the meal following the services for your gathered family at the church reception hall. If there is anything else we can do to be of comfort, please let us know at any hour.

With love and sympathy,

Don, Patty, Trina, and Tonya

Dear Maria,

We know words are inadequate comfort for the depth of your grief over Austin's choice to end his life. Our thoughts are with you. As parents, we all do the best we know to do in guiding our children. It is all we can do.

We loved Austin and will miss him greatly. Our hope is that the love of the many who care so much about you, Austin, and your family will help soothe your pain.

Sincerely,
Morgan and Kareena

*Morgan & Kareena*

Dear Dean and Adele,

I'm so sad to learn of Anita's passing. Perhaps the words of Helen Keller will bring you comfort:

"What we have deeply loved
we can never lose
for all we love deeply,
becomes a part of us."

In sympathy, Lonnie

## Loss through suicide, condolence to best friends:

*Dear Lynn and Todd,*

*It was with a heavy heart that I read about Damen in the obituaries today.*

*It is impossible to find words to ease your anguish. There is no way to be prepared for such a thing or the enormity of the despair.*

*We can only recall all of the joy Damen brought into our lives through the time and activities we shared with him.*

*We love you so much and would do anything to bring you comfort, if only we knew what to do.*

*Perhaps this summer you two would like to spend a few days at our cabin, with or without us, to reflect upon all the fine qualities about Damen and to restore your joy through nature.*

*Love,*

*Chuck and Darlene*

## CHAPTER NINE

# Loss of a Pet

*F*or many people, a pet provides comfort, unconditional love, and companionship. Some consider pets to be their best friends, and they may have the same intensity of feeling for them as for family members. Since titles are another way of defining bonding, and bonding is one more way of explaining an emotional relationship, to say a pet is just an animal is to say a friend is just a person. Be sensitive to that quality of bond.

Relationships are not based on who we are, but who we are to each other. It is a well-documented fact that many pets have not only enriched but actually saved the lives of their human companions.

When a cherished pet passes away, grief can be quite profound. Loneliness is a major factor for those with only pets for companionship. Because pets can require a great deal of caregiving, with great quantities of emotional rewards given in return, their losses can be devastating. Simply put, love plus loss equals grief, no matter what form that loss may take.

The same steps of grief associated with other types of loss apply to the death of a pet. Anger and discouragement and a sense of abandonment are particularly difficult challenges for children, the elderly, and for those whose safety may depend upon the companionship of a specially trained dog, such as a seeing-eye or hearing-ear dog. Whether a bird, horse, gerbil, cat, fish, dog, or any other sort of pet dies, it is up to the person who experiences the loss to define its meaning for them.

## Loss of a pet dog, condolence to a neighbor:

### The Hartmans

Dear Mr. Miskin,

We were sorry to hear about your dog, Licorice. We always saw you walking him up and down the street and your joy was ours too. We wanted to let you know that our deepest thoughts of sympathy are with you at this time. We hope you'll continue your walks and stop by for a glass of iced tea.

Your neighbors,
Marty and Polly

Dear Michelle,

We know how devastating the need to have Peetie put to sleep was for you. It was a decision only you could make in his best interest, suffering as he was. We're certain his loss as your constant companion brings not only pain but fresh recognition of just what a special dog friend he always was, not to mention a fisherman in his own right!

Thank you for sharing his joys with us over the years on fishing and camping trips, outings when he ate all the hot dogs, and evenings when he dreamed and snored by the fire as we laughed and played cards until all hours. We shall all miss Peetie.

Love, Tina and Allen

## Loss of a pet dog, condolence to a young man:

*The*

*Stephens*

Dear David,

   This must be a difficult time for you and everyone involved. Please know that while you have made a courageous decision to ease Button's suffering, it was no doubt a painful choice to have to make. We think of you in your time of loss.

Sincerely,
Kelly and Ruby

## Loss of a pet dog, condolence to a young woman:

Dear Carol,

   Black Jewel meant so much to you. Knowing she was there for you during good times and hard ones, I can appreciate the sadness you feel in losing your most devoted companion.

   My thoughts of sorrow and concern are with you. May peace be yours in the days ahead. I will be in touch next week to see if you'd like to go for a hike on the weekend.

With deepest sympathy,
Marla

## Loss of a pet horse, condolence to a couple:

Dear Skip and Julie,

We were shocked to hear that Sorel's Dream had to be put down after her fall at Steeple Chase practice. You've talked of little else but getting her ready for the autumn equestrian events, so the thought of Skip being unable to compete with her this coming season, after months of diligent training, is too sad for words.

Our thoughts are with you in this difficult time for your family, your equestrian team, and for the many fans, like ourselves, of your beautiful quarter horse.

We know our words are inadequate to express what we hope would bring you comfort, yet we felt impelled to let you know how we sympathize sincerely with your feelings at her loss.

With deep affection and sympathy,

Brian and Hope

and the children,

Kassy and KC

## Loss of a pet horse, condolence to a friend:

Dear Stacey,

I was so sorry to get a phone call this morning from Tim, saying your beautiful Arabian, Chestnut, contracted an illness and had to be put to sleep. Since your phone is ringing busy, I'll take a moment to try and find words to send you some bit of comfort. You must feel sadder than I can imagine to lose Chestnut.

I've watched you raise him from a colt, and spend many hours spoiling him, training him to barrel race, and riding him proudly in our posse events.

I get off work early on Friday afternoons, so I'll call and see if you'd like a little company, or help with his tack or cleaning his stall, the way we've always done it together before rodeo and posse events.

Stacey, I'm so sorry. My heart is breaking for you.

Love,
Dianne

**Loss of a pet kitten, condolence to a friend's family:**

*M*

Dear Sue Ann, Ray, Mitzy, and Paul,

We were so sorry to hear of the loss of your adorable kitten, Slippers. She was such an exceptional little beauty and we know how you all doted upon her four white feet and perky disposition. Slippers stole all of our hearts with her pouncing after everything that moved and curling into a mound of fluff to take a nap. I'm so glad we took movies of your family with her when you first brought her over to introduce her on Mitzy's birthday. We'll have a copy made for your dear memories of her.

It's hard to comfort a child at the loss of a precious pet, because we grown-ups have a tough time when our pets have a tragic end, too. We extend our sorrow to everyone in your family at this sad time.

We're going camping for a week on the 20th. Please discuss whether or not Mitzy and Paul could join us as a way of having something positive to look forward to in their sadness. This is the year the kids get their own fishing gear and they'll be eager to share what they learn with their friends.

Love,

Rob, Jenny, John, and Gina

## Loss of a pet parrot, condolence to a friend:

Dear Nicki,

Thank you for letting me know about Preston. It's impossible to imagine your apartment without that sassy parrot shrieking in the background whenever we play and sing the high notes on the piano.

I'm so sorry to learn that his quietness and feather loss meant he was terminally sick. You have been companions for so long that it must be a difficult adjustment to not have his welcoming "Where the 'L' have you been, Sweetie?" greet you when you open the door. I'm certainly going to miss it and remember him with a smile.

Please call to talk when you feel overwhelmed with the quiet. We can talk of all the great times we shared with Preston and the antics he performed now and then for getting out to fly around your kitchen.

Love,
Jeannie

## Loss of pet gerbils, condolence to a niece:

Dear Amber,

We are sorry your gerbils got out and Tabby Ann found them first. You've taken such good care of your pets, I know you must feel so sad. It's nature's way that cats chase mice and gerbils, so try to not blame yourself or your cat. When you feel ready for a new gerbil, Uncle Russ and I will take you to the pet store for another one and buy a clip latch for safety, too. We love you, honey, and are hoping you know we care.

Love, Aunt Cass and Uncle Russ

## CHAPTER TEN

# Preparing a Eulogy &
# Eulogy Examples

*T*he written eulogy is a fine tribute in praise of someone who has died, usually presented as a reading at a gathering of relatives and friends. Delivered in a calm and kind manner, the eulogy, or a number of them, generally focuses on the praiseworthy attributes of the deceased.

Occasionally, it is not uncommon these days for the legendary interests or less-than-criminal vices of the person to be recounted in a loving fashion for the comforting amusement of those in attendance. Such "reality" makes for a bond of recognition of family stories that all are familiar with and that make the funeral or memorial event seem less impersonal.

References to Uncle Norm and his infamous cigar, the way Grandma Sadie cursed in Danish—only—each time the dog dug under the fence and got away, or that Uncle Charlie liked to play the horses are in the realm of warm family humor.

Avoid referring to family- or business-private matters, as people might be embarrassed or perhaps irreparably hurt financially, emotionally, in their relationships, or spiritually.

It is wise for the eulogist to take time to discuss their desired approach with key family members, business partners, or close friends so that no one is surprised or offended at such remarks.

The eulogy is a way to express your love one more time. It is important in the healing process. It expresses joy, sorrow, laughter, and tears.

It is difficult if not impossible for one eulogy to sum up one person's entire personality, spirit, and accomplishments. If several people are asked to eulogize a deceased loved one, friend, or coworker, the family making the request should clearly define the area of life each eulogizer is to be responsible for celebrating in their tribute.

## How to Use Eulogy Examples

*W*hen a eulogy writer is experiencing strong emotions of their own that may be as intense as the bereaved people gathered to honor the deceased, it is often helpful for that person to have examples to peruse for what to say. Eulogies are often printed in newsletters, newspapers, organization updates, and even published in books—depending upon how well known the deceased person was—so spending time to prepare remarks in the appropriate "flavor" of the deceased and their legacy will give the family and the eulogist comfort. Tender admiration can be beautifully expressed.

Eulogy examples to follow vary from quite formal perhaps in an historical approach to warmly casual and conversational with the purpose of assisting those who need tender ways to express their admiration for a loved one, friend, business associate, or distant relative who has died.

Select a phrase, a paragraph, a poem, or an idea to make your own written eulogy of homage to someone as personal as you like. It is perfectly appropriate to include a reference to the original in your remarks.

For example, you might say something to this effect: When Thomas Jefferson eulogized his colleague President George Washington, he said . . . which sums up the way I feel about Grandfather Edwards and his commitment to his ideals.

# Examples of Eulogies

**Excerpts from eulogies for President of the United States, George Washington**
**by President Thomas Jefferson**

"Perhaps the strongest feature in George Washington's character was prudence, never acting until every circumstance, every consideration, was maturely weighed; refraining if he saw a doubt, but, when once decided, going through with his purpose, whatever obstacles opposed.

"His integrity was most pure, his justice the most inflexible. His temper was naturally high toned; but reflection and resolution had obtained a firm and habitual ascendancy over it. If ever, however, it broke its bonds, he was most tremendous in his wrath. . . .

"His person, you know, was fine, his stature exactly what one would wish, his deportment easy, erect and noble; the best horseman of his age, and the most graceful figure that could be seen on horseback. . . .

". . . truly it may be said that never did nature and fortune combine more perfectly to make a man great . . . of which the history of the world furnishes no other example. . . ."

**by President Abraham Lincoln**

"This is the one hundred and tenth anniversary of the birthday of [President George] Washington. . . . On that name, a eulogy is expected.

"It cannot be. To add brightness to the sun, or glory to the name of Washington, is alike impossible. Let none attempt it. In solemn awe pronounce the name, and in its naked deathless splendor, leave it shining on."

**Excerpts from eulogies for President of the United States, John F. Kennedy**
**by Mike Mansfield, Majority Leader of the U.S. Senate**

". . . In death he gave of himself to us. He gave us of a good heart from which the laughter came. He gave us of a profound wit, from which a great leadership emerged. He gave us of a kindness and a strength fused into a human courage to seek peace without fear.

"He gave us of his love that we, too, in turn, might give. He gave that we might give of ourselves, that we might give to one another until there would be no room, no room at all, for the bigotry, the hatred, prejudice, and the arrogance which converged in that moment of horror to strike him down."

**by Earl Warren, Chief Justice of the United States**

"There is nothing that adds shock to our sadness as the assassination of our leader, chosen as he is to embody the ideals of our people, the faith we have in our institutions and our belief in the fatherhood of God and the brotherhood of man. . . .

"We are saddened; we are stunned; we are perplexed.

"John Fitzgerald Kennedy, a great and good President, the friend of all men of good will, a believer in the dignity and equality of all human beings, a fighter for justice, an apostle of peace, has been snatched from our midst by the bullet of an assassin. . . .

"Our Nation is bereaved. The whole world is poorer because of his loss. But we can all be better Americans because John Fitzgerald Kennedy has passed our way, because he has been our chosen leader at a time in history when his character, his vision, and his quiet courage have enabled him to chart for us a safe course through the shoals of treacherous seas that encompass the world."

**Excerpts from eulogies for President of the United States, John F. Kennedy**
**by John W. McCormack, Speaker of the House of Representatives**

" . . . While this is an occasion of deep sorrow it should be also one of dedication. We must have the determination to unite and carry on the spirit of John Fitzgerald Kennedy for a strengthened America and a future world of peace.

**by Senator Jacob Javits**

". . . I am a personal witness to the fact that [John Fitzgerald Kennedy] was resourceful, optimistic, and creative. He became and was my friend, and this is a deep source of gratification to me and to Mrs. Javits and our family. . . .

"He was vigorous and healthy and smiling and friendly—a complete human being, concerned about other human beings who were no longer as vigorous and not quite as healthy as they used to be.

"This concern for the unfortunate . . . with all of the social graces and all the social status and as much power as America allows one man was what made him so much the symbol of the youth of our country."

**Excerpt from a eulogy for Pierre Elliot Trudeau, Prime Minister of Canada**
**by Justin Trudeau [his son]**

". . . Pierre Elliot Trudeau. The very words convey so many things to so many people. . . . Statesman, intellectual, professor, adversary, outdoorsman, lawyer, journalist, author, Prime Minister of Canada. But more than anything, to me, he was dad. And what a dad. He loved us with the passion and the devotion that encompassed his life. He taught us to believe in ourselves, to stand up for ourselves, to know ourselves, and to accept responsibility for ourselves. . . .

"We have gathered from coast to coast to coast, from one ocean to another, united in our grief, to say goodbye. . . .

". . . he won't be coming back anymore. It's all up to us, all of us, now.

"The woods are lovely, dark and deep. He has kept his promises and earned his sleep.

*"Je t'aime Papa."*

## Excerpts from eulogies for Prime Minister Rabin of Israel by President Hosni Mubarak of Egypt

"It is with deep regret that we are assembled here today to pay our last regrets to Prime Minister Yitzhak Rabin, a courageous leader and recognized statesman . . . his untimely loss . . . at this important juncture in the history of the Middle East has dealt a severe blow to our noble cause. . . . On this sad occasion, ladies and gentlemen, I extend the condolences of the government of Egypt and my personal condolences to the government of Israel and the family of Yitzhak Rabin."

## by King Hussein of Jordan

"I never thought that the moment would come like this, when I would grieve the loss of a brother, a colleague and a friend, a man, a soldier who met us on the opposite side of a divide, whom we respected as he respected us, a man I came to know because I realized as he did that we had to cross over the divide, establish the dialogue and strive to leave also for us a legacy that is worthy of him.

". . . You lived as a soldier. You died as a soldier for peace and I believe it is time for all of us to come out openly and to speak of peace. Not here today, but for all the times to come. . . .

"... We believe that our one God wishes us to live in peace and wishes peace upon us. Let's not keep silent.

"... He was a man of courage, a man of vision and he was endowed with one of the greatest virtues that any man can have . . . humility.

"The peaceful people in the majority of my country, of the armed forces and people who once were your enemies are somber today and their hearts are heavy.

"Let us hope and pray that God will give us all guidance each in his respective position to do what he can for the better future that Yitzhak Rabin sought."

**Excerpt from a eulogy for Prime Minister Yitzhak Rabin by Noa Ben-Artzi Filosof [his granddaughter]**

"You will forgive me, for I do not want to talk about peace. I want to talk about my grandfather. . . .

"Grandfather, you were, and still are, our hero. I want you to know that in all I have ever done, I have always seen you before my eyes. Your esteem and love accompanied us in every step and on every path, and we lived in the light of your values.

"You never abandoned us, and now they have abandoned you. . . . I am incapable of finishing, but it appears that a strange hand, a miserable person, has already finished for me. . . . Having no choice, I part from you, a hero, and ask that you rest in peace, that you think about us and miss us, because we here—down below—love you so much.

"I have no feelings of revenge because my pain and loss are so big, too big. We will love you grandfather, always."

**Excerpts from a eulogy for Princess Diana, former wife of Prince Charles of the United Kingdom by Earl Charles Spencer [her brother]**

". . . We are all united not only in our desire to pay our respects to Diana but rather our need to do so. . . . Diana was the very essence of compassion, of duty, of style, of beauty. All over the world she was a symbol of selfless humanity. . . . Today is our chance to say thank you for the way you brightened our lives. . . . We will all feel cheated always that you were taken from us so young and yet we must learn to be grateful that you came along at all. . . .

"To sanctify your memory would be to miss out on the very core of your being, your wonderfully mischievous sense of humour with a laugh that bent you double . . . and a boundless energy which you could barely contain.

"For all the status, the glamour, the applause, Diana remained throughout a very insecure person at heart, almost childlike in her desire to do good for others so she could release herself from deep feelings of unworthiness of which her eating disorders were merely a symptom. The world sensed this part of her character and cherished her for her vulnerability whilst admiring her for her honesty. . . .

"I would like to end by thanking God for the small mercies he has shown us at this dreadful time. For taking Diana at her most beautiful and radiant and when she had joy in her private life.

"Above all we give thanks for the life of a woman I am so proud to be able to call my sister, the unique, the complex, the extraordinary and irreplaceable Diana whose beauty, both internal and external, will never be extinguished from our minds."

**Excerpt from a eulogy for Wilma Louise Miller
by Susie McGruder McGlish [her daughter]**

"I'm grateful for my mom being there for me when we were left without my dad. She held life together for my brother and for me. Never one to give much in the way of affection, which seemed to make her quite uncomfortable, she gave in other ways. She was a terrific cook and loved to try unusual ingredients, always with great success.

"Later, after my stepfather died, she cooked professionally in a restaurant and made a decent living for herself. She had quite a following among long-haul truck drivers, of which she was very proud because she always said, 'Those fellas are always hungry and they'll return to a place where the food makes them feel like they're already back home.'

"Mom opened the world of reading for knowledge and for pleasure and introduced me to critical thinking. She listened and read avidly and could converse intelligently on most any topic. She made me want to learn.

"She was a collector of antique furniture and decorative items and though her day was before computers, she would research the history of the objects she found pleasing and be able to explain their provenance with enthusiasm.

"My mother was also your friend. She probably called you on the phone to see how you were feeling after a bout with the flu. Or she shared a pot of one of her ever-simmering stews or a beautiful card she had made herself. She might have come by your porch and anonymously left you a Mason® jar of roses from her garden. She cared about you. She cared about me. She cared about her family. She was not yours, she was not mine— she belonged to God and has gone to live with Him."

**Excerpts from eulogies for Mimi Fariña [musical group] by Paul Liberatore [her partner]**

"I'm Paul Liberatore, and for the past four years, I have had the honor, privilege, and great good fortune of being Mimi Fariña's partner, soul mate, caregiver, lover, and friend.

". . . of all the treatments over the past two years, the one that seemed to have done her the most good was dancing. Every week for as long as she was physically able, she attended Anna Halprin's Moving Toward Life class, using dance, drawing, visualization, poetry, and other arts in her courageous effort to heal. . . . Mimi and I had to deal with the terrible paradox of hoping for the best while preparing for the worst.

"She had to accept the possibility that she would, in her words, have to leave the planet before she was ready.

"After Mimi died, I found another piece of her artwork she'd done in her dance class and left for me . . . a drawing of a bold dancer, a tall, proud, grand woman in a winged robe and long flowing hair, holding a feather to the heavens. The drawing came with a poem she had written titled *Follow Me.* This is what it said:

*Follow me*

> *The wind, the eagle feather*

*Follow me*

> *Let me lead*

*Dance the cancer*

> *Relinquish the fear*

*The sky will twirl open*

> *The sky will twirl open*

> > *The sky will twirl open.*"

## Excerpt from a eulogy for Mimi Fariña
by Lana Sevem [her friend]

"In an interview, Mimi said, 'I could see the need to bring music to people who are confined or suffering or not in touch with the outside world. You don't have to preach . . . , you just have to be there and make the music. It gets through on another level than medication or punishment . . . the whole work of Bread & Roses, performing for convicts in prison, seniors who are isolated, children in kids' wards who many never come back out . . . I try to make some sort of community for them.'

"The positive thing about the burning out of a star in the universe is that you continue to perceive its light for, possibly, millions of years. I believe this is the case with Mimi, her work will span many generations from now *ad infinitum.*

"I would like to rededicate my willingness to perform and contribute to her work.

"As Bread & Roses goes forward, setting the stage for human kindness, Mimi will be there. She will always be its shining star, its guiding light."

## Eulogy for Joanie Lundsted
by Lars Lundsted [her brother]

"I thought I'd worked this out after Joanie died. People have to die. Or else, with all the sex and having babies that goes on, it would get too crowded. We'd run out of food, room and money. Running out of food, for a great cook like Joanie, would really be no good, no way to spoil anybody at her table. I don't know if the question 'Why?' ever really goes away when we lose someone we love. But I know what really helps for me is remembering that before Joanie died—she really lived."

## Excerpts from eulogies for Thomas Ungar
## by Ruthy Rosenfeld

"Whoever met Thomas and became his friend always knew what a marvelous gift he was given. I would like to speak of Thomas our friend, and the uncle and friend of our daughters Noa and Yael. Clever and handsome, amusing and curious, sweet and kindhearted. . . . Wild and serious, disciplined and colourful, a man who was a stranger to the word banality, with whom you were never bored. His presence filled a room when he entered it, and the room would burst at the seams when Nurit and the kids joined in for a meal. To this day, my grown-up daughters remember and long for the stories he told them.

"In one of our last exchanges, about a week ago, he said apologetically, 'You see, I come and go.' Now that he will no longer come, I can't help recalling the night of the Seder (Passover dinner ceremony) and the Beretzky's in Even Yehuda, when we made him read his bit of the Hagada, like everyone else, and heard his thundering singing voice.

*And all that only four months ago,*

*but all of it—forever.*

*You will live in my memory."*

## by Yona Rosenfeld

". . . All we can do here and now is to allow different people to surprise us with their Thomas, with another and yet another aspect of him, and even these won't help us to overcome that terrible sense of what we have lost, and the wonderful feeling of what this unique man had meant to us.

". . . When Rilke, one of the poets whom Thomas liked, died—it was said that it upset the order of the universe. . . .

"For us, the universe without Thomas will never be the same again."

**A Tribute to Gerald Yablans**
**by Stanley Goldsmith**

"Gerry was a friend, a caring generous friend who didn't wait to be asked to help someone; he volunteered assistance. He didn't brag about what he had done. He usually was silent about it to preserve the pride and dignity of whomever he was helping. He wanted no applause.

"In this Synagogue, at Friday night services that he attended regularly, he sat in the last row. I asked him why did he do that?, he told me he wasn't there to be seen. . . .

"We jogged together for over 20 years; we probably jogged a total of 25,000 miles, the distance around the world at the equator. While jogging we talked about life, family, religion, politics, philanthropy, business, medicine, movies, plays, books. He always listened intently. When it came to this terrible final episode, he said, 'Look, it is what it is; I just want the best shot at treatment—even if it all ends abruptly; I just want to be in the game, to know that I gave it my best shot; that I am not   sitting helplessly on the sideline.' Gerry Yablans kept the commandments. He sustained and enriched many lives."

**Excerpt from a eulogy for his grandmother**
**by Chief Sean Joseph Wolfe**

"You have departed this earthly life, but not our hearts and memories."

**Excerpt from a eulogy for his mother**
**by Chief Matumbo Effiong**

"Your children will recall your name with pride for many generations to come—as countless as the stars."

**Excerpt from the Service of Celebration
for the Life of Patti Harper Coyle
by Dan Coyle [her husband]**

"In the days ahead we hope to think less about all we've lost and grow more thankful for all we gained from knowing and loving Patti. We hope this service helps to move us toward that place.

"We want this to be a 'thumbs up' service. During her illness Patti responded to the most discouraging medical news by turning to family members and giving them a 'thumbs up' sign. At various points in this service family members may feel compelled to offer up a thumbs-up salute to Patti. . . . Please join them.

"Patti left us so suddenly that when we learned that she was sick, we said to ourselves, 'She has done so much for me—what have I done for her?' We all need to rid ourselves of those thoughts, not just because they're unhealthy but because they're so wrongheaded. It would be very difficult to outperform Patti in acts of love and kindness. She would not let you. You could not out-Patti Patti. As her husband, I gave up keeping score long ago after it became clear that I would always be an Avis to her Hertz. I would try harder, but I would always be a Number 2.

"The response of family and friends to her illness has overwhelmed us. The cards, the phone calls, the services offered and provided let Patti know how deeply she was loved by those who knew her. Our heartfelt thanks to all of you. In the words of William Butler Yeats, modified for this occasion:

*Think where human glory most begins and ends*

*and say her glory was she had such friends."*

# Excerpts from Anonymous Eulogies

## Excerpts from anonymous eulogies for deceased brothers

"My brother saw good in everyone. He taught us all the meaning of tolerance and forgiveness. It is up to us to practice the lessons he was with us to teach."

"He's gone home to be an angel as he was to our family on earth."

"My baby brother, 6 foot 5 and bigger than life, you were always the one I could look up to. May you rest in peace. No time or space can erase your image and importance to us."

## Excerpts from anonymous eulogies for deceased fathers

"Dad, you were my idol. You taught me well. It is my turn to pass on your lessons to my children and grandchildren."

"You were a loving responsible man."

"We remember you as a dedicated husband and father."

"Pop, your suffering is over. Sleep on in the arms of Jesus. We shall meet again in heaven."

"Cherished father, until we meet again, Shalom."

## Excerpts from anonymous eulogies for suicide deaths

"May she find the peace in heaven that she could not find, even with our determined and loving efforts, in life on earth."

"Ours is not to explain or perhaps even to understand, but to go on loving his memory and living the life on his behalf that he so wanted for himself and could not achieve."

## CHAPTER ELEVEN

# Preparing an Obituary &
# Obituary Examples

*I*n many regions of the country, it is customary to have the obituary read at the funeral or memorial service. For that reason, the person asked to prepare an obituary may want to read their rough draft aloud to hear how it will "sound" to gathered mourners as well as how it will read in the newspaper.

Obituary notices must be verified by the mortuary. It is important to note than an obituary is the public notice of a death with the facts and as much warmth and personality as the family cares to invest in newspaper column length. A three or four paragraph obituary column will cost $85 to $100 or more for each newspaper in which it appears. People are often surprised that there is a modest charge for these publishing services by their local newspaper. The obituary is also often published in the newsletters of the organizations to which the deceased was an active member and may, as well, be posted on a web site.

An obituary has basic components that are fairly standard worldwide, while the style or "voice" of approaching what is said may be traditional to a local, social, or religious culture or community. Among the facts concerning a deceased person's life that an obituary preparer should collect before writing are:

• full name of the deceased. Include first, last, middle, maiden, and married (however many times) as gender form is appropriate.

• age.

• address at time of death.

• date of death, the day and date.

• place of death, whether at home, in hospital, while traveling, etc. One may disclose cause if desired, such as: "died of injuries sustained in an auto, hunting, biking, climbing accident," "passed away of causes incident to age," "succumbed after a valiant battle with cancer," "was taken from us due to complications at birth."

• names of parents.

• date of birth, day and year.

• current spouse's name, marriage date, place of marriage. A former spouse's name and date of divorce or death.

• education.

• church affiliation and services rendered.

• organizations, social clubs, offices held if applicable.

• military service, service branch, dates, conflicts, achieved officer status, career honors.

• places lived.

• career history or business/professional/or work-related information, including level or job achievement, retired, etc.

• survivors: spouse, sons and daughters, grandchildren, parents, grandparents, brothers and sisters.

- funeral, graveside, or memorial services by date, time, and location.

- visitation with family, with or without the deceased's body present by date, time, and location.

- interment (burial) if private family service or if open to co-workers and friends, date, time, and location.

- the family requests, in lieu of flowers, donations in [the deceased's name] may be sent to . . . fund, foundation, charity.

## How to Use Obituary Examples

*S*elect a phrase, a paragraph, a poem, or an idea from the sample obituaries to make your own obituary for someone you've lost through death as personal as you like. It is perfectly appropriate to include a reference to the original obituary in your own write up, if the reference is to a well-known person with whom the readers and listening mourners at a funeral service will be able to identify.

## Examples of Obituaries

### Excerpt from an obituary for Dr. Albert Schweitzer

Lambarene, Gabon, Sept. 6, 1965

Doctor Albert Schweitzer, 90, died last night at 11:30 P.M. in his jungle hospital here. Death was attributed to circulatory trouble brought on by his advanced age. Albert Schweitzer was born at Kaystersberg, Haute Alçase, Jan. 14th, 1875. He was the son of a Lutheran pastor.

He was buried in a brief and simple ceremony early this afternoon next to an urn containing the ashes of his wife, Helene, who died in Europe in 1957. The grave, on the banks of the Ogooue River, is marked by a cross he made himself. Hospital workers, lepers, and other patients gathered as the body of the noted physician, scholar, philosopher, theologian, winner of the Nobel Peace Prize for his work in Africa, author, and accomplished musician was lowered into the ground. Schweitzer himself once counseled: "You must give some time to your fellowman, even if it's a little thing, do something for those who have need of a man's help, something for which you get no pay but the privilege of doing it."

He took the search for the good life seriously. For him it had profound religious implications. Schweitzer lived his philosophy of reverence for life in regard to plants and animals as well as his fellow man.

**Excerpt from an obituary for Leslie Thomas Vause, male, Navy veteran** (A flag image may be requested to appear with the picture of the deceased, when he or she is an armed forces veteran.)

Leslie Thomas Vause, 87, died Sunday, September 15, 2001, in Baltimore, MD of causes incident to age. He was born July 28, 1919, in Chicago, IL, to Nina Anne Breski and Theodore Lane Vause. His schooling was completed in Baltimore.

He served in the U.S. Navy, 1943–46, as a gunnery officer in the Pacific and returned to civilian life as a bank teller in Baltimore. He rose to head loan officer of First Federal Savings and Loan and served in that capacity until his retirement.

He married Luella Lindstrom in Baltimore in 1938. They had three children: Stella (Bradley) Moulton, Dean (Sarah), and the late Julene (Andrew) Lingley.

He was preceded in death by his parents, his daughter Julene, and his brother Ralph. He is survived by his wife, two children Stella and Dean, seven grandchildren, and twenty-three great grandchildren.

He was a lifetime member of the Order of Elks and rose to the high office of Grand Master of his lodge.

Friends may call on the family from 6–8 P.M. on Tuesday and Wednesday evenings at the Loftgrin Funeral home.

Funeral services will be held on Thursday morning, September 19th, at 11 A.M.

## Excerpt from an obituary for Angela Adams, infant

Three-day-old baby Angela died of a heart valve abnormality on May 3, 2002. She is survived by her parents Raymond and Jennifer (Sweetly) Adams. Graveside services will be held Thursday May 7th at Fairlawn Cemetary. No Visitation is planned. In lieu of flowers, donations may be made in Angela's name to the Primary Children's Hospital of Lancaster, PA.

## Excerpt from an obituary for Bernita Clark Brenneman, accident victim

Bernita Clark Brenneman, 42, died Wednesday, March 9, 2002, of injuries resulting from an auto-pedestrian accident in Smith County on Highway 39.

Bernita "Bitzy" Clark was born August 27, 1960, in Buffalo, NY, to Dwight and Annalee Clark.

She was the wife of Howard Brenneman. They were married 31 years ago in rural upstate New York.

Bernita graduated magna cum laude from Bowling Green State University of Ohio, and went on to achieve her masters degree in vocal music from Ohio University. She taught music in the public schools of Buffalo for 18 years. Many of her students went on to careers in the field of music. She was an inspiring teacher with a proud following.

She is survived by her mother, her husband Dwight, one daughter Cassandra, two sisters Alicia (Brian) Anderson and Twila Clark, three nieces, and two nephews.

Friends may call at the Norton Funeral Home on Friday evening between 6–8 P.M. Services are graveside on Saturday morning, March 12, 2002.

A music scholarship in Bernita's name has been established with the First Security and Trust Bank, to be awarded to outstanding students in vocal music at Fremont High School. The fund will be administered through the school and the award finalist will be selected from among the annual nominees by the Clark and Anderson families.

## Obituary for David George Gilchrist

David George Gilchrist was born August 21, 1953, in Spokane, WA, to Darrel and Barbara Gilchrist. He died at Phillips Regional Hospital on July 5, 2002, of heart failure.

David graduated with honors from Altamore High School and went on to earn a Batchelor of Science degree from Oregon State University. He returned to Spokane and married his high-school sweetheart Mary Jo Humphries, with whom he reared three surviving sons: George Andrew (Beth Anne) Gilchrist, Darrel Welsley Gilchrist, and Daniel David Gilchrist.

Mary Jo and David's sons will continue to operate the family fresh produce truck farm business, begun in 1987.

David loved to play baseball and was an avid golfer with his sons. He cherished every day and made life a joy for his beloved family. He shall be missed by all who knew him.

He was preceded in death by his father and one sister, Joyce (Brad) Anderson.

Graveside services will be held Monday, July 9, 2002, at Hilpert Cemetery, 5200 South on Wilshire. Friends and family may call prior to services from 11:00 to 12:30 A.M. at Boye's Mortuary, 3765 Vista Ave.

In lieu of flowers, it was David's express wish that contributions be made to the University of Washington's Heart Research Institute in Spokane, WA.


## Excerpt from an obituary for Miriam Gilbert Rasmussen

Miriam Gilbert Rasmussen, 74, passed away Thursday, May 11, 2002, at her town home, after a long battle with cancer.

She was born August 30, 1928, in Atlanta, GA, to John Ross Gilbert and Betty Blue Hollingsworth. She married Eugene M. Rasmussen in 1948. He died in 1991.

She was a faithful member of the St. Paul's Episopal church her entire life and taught Sunday School for 37 years.

She is survived by two sons, Bruce Rasmussen, and Scott (Amy) Rasmussen of Buena Vista and their five children who will miss their "Grand Nanna's" trips for ice cream cones.

## CHAPTER TWELVE

# Voiced Words of Comfort

*I*n the event that you meet someone on the street or at a formal gathering, such as at a funeral, memorial service, wake, social, or organizational event, it is important to you and the bereaved person that you express some fitting verbal condolence.

Putting your sincere sympathy into words on paper may be easier, as it is once-removed from dealing directly with a grieving person's emotions as well as your own; however, voicing words of comfort is an act of concern and healing for you both.

Whether at the family's home following a service or in a chance meeting, or any of the occasions mentioned above, it is far less awkward than ignoring a death if you have something kind and sensitive to say. It doesn't matter how brief your remarks are to bring comfort to a business associate, friend, or family member who is suffering loss through a death. The important thing is to voice your sorrow to a grieving person you know in their loss. They will appreciate just knowing they are thought of and wished well in their grieving process.

Borrow phrases from previous condolence-note examples in this book, or use those to follow that are comfortable for you to express personally, in a one-on-one situation, a genuine voicing of your concern.

It is perfectly appropriate to use the three Rs of recognition, remembrance, and reassurance as topic approaches to include in what you choose to say.

Keep in mind the three Rs as suggested throughout this book:

**Recognition**

**Remembrance**

**Reassurance**

• **Recognition:** It is not necessary to ask for or to retell what you may have read or been told by someone else concerning the death a person is grieving over. This is particularly important if the death was sudden, pertained to a child, was of a gruesome nature, or was the result of a suicide. What is necessary is to express your heartfelt sympathy as directly and briefly as possible to that grieving person.

*Martha, Tim and I are so saddened to hear about your father's recent passing. His loss must be very painful for you.*

Ordinarily, the bereaved person with whom you are speaking will acknowledge with a simple "Thank you," unless the person is needing to talk. Then, if you have the time, being a good listener may be the greatest comfort you can provide. If they change the subject, stay on the new one with them. If there is an awkward silence, you might say something from among the remembrance or reassurance categories.

• **Remembrance:** Respond with or initiate a brief tribute to some memorable anecdote or fine quality of the deceased.

*Martha, we remember fondly how much your father loved to fish for trout every time he had the opportunity. He was a master at it and I'm sure your children have many wonderful memories of being taught how to cast by an expert.*

✥

*Your dad was always so kind to my children. He made every visit memorable with his gentle teasing that seemed to make each of the girls feel special to him in their own unique way.*

*Terry, I was so sorry to hear that your niece did not survive her accident injuries. Please accept my deepest sympathy.*

*Mrs. Goodwin, our family was saddened to hear about Mr. Goodwin's passing. The two of you have served us so well over the many years we've been shopping at your meat market. He will be warmly remembered for his cheerful greeting and thoughtfulness.*

• **Reassurance:** Let grieving adults and children know as you meet, that your thoughts or prayers are with them. If you know them well, offer to help in some specific way. Do not put the grieving person on the spot by expecting her or him to bring up the death topic first. Bereaved people are under tremendous stress. Make your communication as easy on them as possible.

*Ginger, I just heard that your mother was taken ill suddenly and passed on. You have my sincere sympathy. She was my children's favorite Halloween treat stop. Her yard is the biggest one on the block. I wonder if you would like help keeping it mowed for a couple of weeks while you're busy with her arrangements.*

*Danny, the passing of your infant son must be more painful than I can imagine. With Karine recuperating and grieving, perhaps you would appreciate a couple of casseroles that you could just warm up for your family. Tell me what the children like and I'll make them.*

*Nicole, I'm sure you must feel very upset about your mom. Things can get confusing when all the big people around you are hurting like you are. She was special and always helped you with your homework.*
*Would you like to come over after school and work on yours while Nathan does his? I'll bake a plate of brownies. We can all help, so you don't get behind while everyone is busy at this time.*

# Additional Phrases of Condolence

## Words of comfort to someone who has lost a mother

*I'm so sorry to hear that your mother has passed on. You can take comfort that she set an example of caring for you and your children. She was always so interested in their activities and accomplishments.*

*Please accept my deepest sympathies in regard to your mother's death. Your mom knew how to make everyone feel so at home the minute they walked in her door. I shall always remember her welcoming hugs and that beautiful smile that greeted me. You have so many of her fine qualities.*

*I've just heard of your mother's passing. I'm so sorry for your loss. Whenever I think of what a mother ought to be like, I will remember yours and how kind she was to me.*

## Words of comfort to someone who has lost a father

*I'm saddened to hear that your father has passed on. Please accept my sincere sympathy for you and your family.*

*When I learned of your dad's passing, I thought of what a kind and generous man he was. Even though this time must be hard for you, you have much to be grateful for by his example. Please accept my heartfelt sympathies.*

## Words of comfort to someone who has lost a child

*I felt so sad to hear of your baby's passing. There is little anyone can say to ease your loss. I'm sure every moment you shared with her is a precious memory.*

*When word came to me that Sally Ann was hurt and did not survive her surgery, I felt so sad for your dear family. If there is something Fred and I can do to help you and Allen or your children through this difficult time, I hope you will tell us.*

*Please accept my condolences in the loss of your nephew. Though I didn't know him, I do know you and how devoted you are to your family. I wish there were something I could do to bring you comfort.*

## Words of comfort to someone who has lost a friend

*I was so sorry when I read that your friend Linda passed away after her long illness. You must miss her very much and yet be relieved that her suffering is at an end and she is at peace.*

*Please accept my sympathies for the loss of your friend Jan.*

## Words of comfort to someone who has lost a pet

*Brad told me that Alfie had to be put to sleep. I'm so sorry for your loss. His daily companionship must have been a great comfort to you.*

# Expressing Sympathy Summary

*P*erhaps the greatest comfort we can bring grieving people is to let them know that the loved one or friend that they lost through death will be cherished in our memory as well as theirs.

Some people need the calming comfort of having their grief acknowledged, their burden of loss or guilt shared, and their fear for the changes death brings eased through specific support. By that I refer to those offers of help with services such as food, shopping, lawn care, letter writing, and scrapbook making. The support of listening, visiting company for the bereaved and alone, and companionship for activities that divert from grief are the personal gestures that are so appreciated by those who have lost loved ones through death.

Sometimes our sincere and brief words can best be supportive by a comforting hug, a quiet walk, the gift of music, or a daily phone call to just check in on someone who is newly alone.

Other more private individuals may prefer to be left alone for a while to deal with their grief without interruption. Respecting their needs to work things out in their own way may be difficult for the compassionate person who likes to take action, but they are essential to the healing process of some individuals.

The gesture you make to help a grieving person find comfort must always take into consideration their personality and their expressed or sensed wishes for how they wish to be approached. Your sincerely expressed sympathy is a comfort gift only you can give to a bereaved person in your own heartfelt words.

# *Index*

Appropriate Salutations, 14–15
Complimentary Closes, 15
Condolence, Additional Phrases of, 92
Condolence Note, Examples, How to Use, 21
Condolence Notes Do's and Don'ts, 20
condolence to:
  best friend, 60, 63, 65–67, 93
  boy or young man, 41
  business partner, 52
  couple, 50–52, 55, 64
  coworker, 51–52, 54
  daughter, 42, 44
  friend, 65-67, 93
  godparents, 38–39
  grandparents, 37–39,
  husband, 26–28
  man, 45, 46, 48, 51, 54, 63
  neighbor, 62
  niece, 67
  parents, 30–36, 38–39, 57–60
  sister, 46
  son, 43
  wife, 23-25
  woman, 45–46, 49, 53–55
Eulogies, Excerpts from Anonymous, 82
eulogy by:
  Baez, Joan, 77
  Coyle, Dan, 81
  Effiong, Matumbo, Chief, 80
  Filosof, Noa, Ben-Artzi, 75
  Goldsmith, Stanley, 80
  Hussein, King, 73–74
  Javits, Jacob, Senator, 72
  Jefferson, Thomas, President 70
  Liberatore, Paul, 78
  Lincoln, Abraham, President, 70
  Lundstedt, Lars, 81
  Mansfield, Mike, Senator, 71
  McCormack, John W., 72
  McGlish, Susie McGruder, 76
  Mubarak, Hosni, President, 73
  Rosenfeld, Ruthy, 80
  Rosenfeld, Yona, 80
  Sevem, Lana, 79
  Spencer, Charles, Earl
  Trudeau, Justin,73
  Warren, Earl, Chief Justice, 71
  Wolfe, Sean Joseph, Chief, 74

Eulogies, Examples of, 70–82
eulogy(ies) for:
  brother, 82
  Coyle, Patti, Harper-, 81
  Diana, Princess, 75
  Fariña, Mimi, 77–78
  fathers, 72–73, 82
  grandmother, 80
  Lundstedt, Joanie, 78
  Kennedy, John F., President, 71–73
  Miller, Wilma Louise, 76
  mother, 80
  Rabin, Yitzhak, Prime Minister, 73–74
  suicide deaths, 79, 82
  Ungar, Thomas, 79
  Trudeau, Pierre Elliot, Prime Minister, 72–73
  Washington, George, President, 70
  Yablans, Gerald, 80
Grief from:
  Adolescent's Perspective, 18
  Child's Perspective, 17
  Man's Perspective, 16
  Woman's Perspective, 16–17
  Young Adult's Perspective, 18
How to:
  Express Sympathy, 10
  Use Condolence Note Examples, 21
  Use Eulogy Examples, 69
  Use Obituary Examples, 85
Loss of a Child, 29–39
  ailing child, 35–36, 93
  child/accidental death, 35
  child/kidnapping/death, 38
  grandchild, 37
  infant, 30, 34, 87, 93
  older child, 39
  miscarriage, 30–32
  stillbirth, 33
Loss of a Friend, Coworker, or Service Person, 47–55
  friend, 48–55
  coworker, 51, 52
  service person, 53–55
Loss of a Parent or Family Member, 40–46
  brother, 45
  father, 41–42
*index continued, 96*

# *Index*

mother, 43–44
   sister, 46
   stepparent, 46
Loss of a Pet, 61–67, 93
   dog, 62–63, 93
   gerbils, 67
   horse, 64–65
   kitten, 66
   parrot, 67
Loss of a Spouse, 22–28
   husband, 23–25
   wife, 26–28
Moodie, Susanna, 9
Obituaries, 83–88
Obituaries, Examples of, 85–88
Obituaries, How to Use Examples, 85
Part One: Bringing Comfort
   to the Grieving, 8–18
   Chapter One: Loss Through Death,
   8–15
   Chapter Two: Defining Perspectives
   & Expressing Sympathy, 16–18
Part Two: Supportive Condolence
   Notes, 19–82
   Chapter Three: Writing Condolence
   Notes, 19–21
   Chapter Four: Loss of a Spouse,
   22–28
   Chapter Five: Loss of a Child, 29–39
   Chapter Six: Loss of a Parent or
   Family Member, 40–46
   Chapter Seven: Loss of a Friend,
   Coworker, or Service Person, 47–55
   Chapter Eight: Loss Through
   Suicide, 56–60
   Chapter Nine: Loss of a Pet, 61–67
Part Three: Tributes to the Deceased,
   68–94
   Chapter Ten: Preparing a Eulogy
   & Eulogy Examples, 68–82
   Chapter Eleven: Preparing an
   Obituary & Obituary Examples,
   83–88
Part Four: Graceful Words, 89–94
   Chapter Twelve: Voiced Words of
   Comfort, 89–94
Schweitzer, Dr. Albert, 86–86

suicide, 56–60, 79
Sympathy, Expressing, Summary, 94
Sympathy, How to Express, 10
Sympathy, When to Express, 10
Sympathy, Defining Perspectives &
   Expressing, 16
Three Rs, Recognition, Remembrance,
   Reassurance, 11–13, 90–91
Writing Condolence Notes, 19–21

## *Photo Credit*

Photos courtesy of PhotoDisc®
Tel. Worldwide: +1 206-441-9355